Choreography as Self-Conditioning — A Written Exhibition

Simone Basani (ed.)

Choreography as Conditioning: introduction to the book series

Choreography as Conditioning is a series of five books conceived and realized in the framework of the artistic research project *Distraction as Discipline*.[1] 'Choreography' is understood here, in a broad sense, as a way of organizing bodies in their surroundings, while 'conditioning' refers to the constraints introduced in a situation in order to become choreographic. What the term 'choreography' points to as well is both the collective character of these processes *(choreo)* and to the generation of diverse kinds of signs *(graphy)*. 'Conditioning' implies the same semantic elements: collectivity *(con)* and the production of in this case linguistic, oral signs *(ditioning* from *dicere,* to say).

Throughout the forty months in which *Distraction as Discipline* has been realized and as one of its constitutive components, different groups of artist researchers have been invited to write *through* their practices, that is, to develop practices of writing departing from the performance of collective artistic/aesthetic research practices in different media. Accordingly, each book in this series addresses different thematic fields on the basis of the intertwined performance of different research practices in different constellations and presents some of the resulting artifacts: a collection of texts.

The ground on which this book series emerges is thus an open-ended, dynamic network of relational practices. The books contribute to this network by fostering an observational attitude in the processes of writing and reading. Instead of being a conclusion of the dynamics that lead to their generation, these

1. *Distraction as Discipline* – An investigation into the function of attention and participation in performance art and art pedagogy / Langsdorf & Luyten 2016 – 2019.

books aim at keeping these dynamics alive and vague enough in order to enable variable insights, open trajectories of sense, and further forms of inquiry. This requires spaces and times for reenacting, revisiting and requestioning, and therefore avoiding non-critical consolidations of preconfigured systems of ideas. In this sense, this book series intends to create conditions for addressing, among many others, the following question: how, where and by whom get things organized and what kinds of spheres of experience are made im/possible by the practices we perform and encounter?

Each book in this series offers different responses to the same invitation: to write *through* practices. For us, as series editors, it is fascinating to see how surprisingly large the range of variations can be. The fourth book, *Choreography as Self-Conditioning,* edited by Simone Basani, presents a "written exhibition". It offers a DIY variation of *House of Ear,* an immersive and introactive sound parcours, conceived and curated by David Helbich and Joris Blanckaert during the fourth working episode of *CASC at KASK.*[2] We want to thank all the contributors for their will to rethink their original works in the context of a book, which entailed finding ways to enact on paper what was originally conceived for an architectural space.

Alex Arteaga & Heike Langsdorf

2. *CASC at KASK* was the title of the cycle of transversal work sessions in which the writing processes which have led to the series *Choreography as Conditioning* (CASC) are rooted. Proposed and organized by Heike Langsdorf within the context of the research trajectory *Distraction as Discipline,* it presented a frame for students, research-collegues and herself to work with invited guests, exploring the notions of 'choreography' and 'conditioning'.

Choreography as Self-Conditioning: introduction to the fourth book

Heike Langsdorf's research raises different questions related to the ecology of artistic practices. I use the term 'ecology' to describe the management of time, memory, attention, and energy by artists within their creation processes.

The series edited by Langsdorf and Arteaga triggers, and creates spaces for further debate regarding ecologies of practicing within and outside networks of artists: how can we welcome each other, both artists and non-artists, within the space of our practices? How could we share our processes and reflections about what we do in an inclusive way? Is this interconnected movement of hosting each other a choreography made of tensions, relations, clashes, gestures, looks, and feelings? Is this the work itself? And still, how long can this choreography last? What kind of spaces does it create while it happens?

In the case of *Choreography as Self-Conditioning*, the space is created by writing. It is a discursive exhibition on paper that follows a performative one called *House of Ear*, presented at *Ear to the Ground Festival*, in 2019. The book's authors are the same makers who had conceived sound works for *House of Ear*. Heike Langsdorf and I have asked them to look back at what they previously created in order to unfold and share a reflection on the role of self-conditioning strategies within their practices.

There is no photo documentation in this written exhibition. Rather, it is the self-reflective discourse of the authors that gives a tour of the pages/exhibition rooms to observe what is left—of the works that comprise *House of Ear*—in their own memory. Every contribution starts with a description of the work reconstructed, indeed, through memory, plus possible additional self-observations that introduce a second part, called *in your hands*.

Here the authors make a cut in the canvas to expose the matter of their practice. The readers are invited to peek, and if they wish, to dive into the cut, engage their bodies with this matter, think *through* it. By taking *in their hands* a set of instructions, do-it-yourself guides, and intimate scores they can access specific spaces for listening. Spaces for listening, and hopefully connecting with impasses, desires, and discoveries of others, the ones experienced firsthand by the authors of the book while developing their practices.

Simone Basani

A Reflection on Composing as Conditioning: practicing towards *House of Ear*

My binary brain has the tendency to subdivide everything into two classes, which are not necessarily in opposition to one another. Likewise, I am used to subdividing music works, as well as the composers who produce them, into two classes, which I label 'representation' and 'presence'.

Representational works exist as soon as the composer has written down their final double barline. These works can be interpreted and reinterpreted under different conditions by other musicians. The audience doesn't necessarily participate in the creation of the work: the answers to the questions posed by the work are provided by the composer.

'Presence' works are totally different (again, it is my binary mind speaking here). The work presented by the composer is always unfinished. It's a proposal and an invitation for the interpreter/s as well as the listener/s to find answers to the questions the work evokes.[3]

Pierre Bourdieu made a distinction between two ways in which an artwork can be understood: the internal reading (i.e. the isolated interpretation of its content), and the external reading (i.e. its correspondence to surrounding social conditions).[4]

3. This explains the very meaning of presence as the act of being: the interpreter/s as well as the listener/s have to be present for the presence work to exist. Consequently, presence works are impossible to reproduce, since that would make them a representation. It is indeed impossible to experience (again) the creation of Stravinsky's *Rite of Spring*, since the scandalous atmosphere it provoked could only exist in combination with anti-Russian and anti-modernist sentiments in Paris at the time. No subsequent reproductions or interpretations were never met with heated conditions like the first creation, which makes the premiere all the more legendary.

Likewise, I would describe representation works as the fruits of internal writing, while presence works result from an external writing process.

Composing a presence work essentially entails generating and predicting conditions for the work to be created. Conditions include: a location, a timing, a timeline, a group of people, social relationships, and societal circumstances. Composition as a practice is understood here much like choreography is explained by Arteaga and Langsdorf: as a way of organizing subjects —musical events, interpreters, and listeners— in their surroundings (that is: in space and time). To stay with the comparison, another instance of *CASC* arises: that of 'Composing as Conditioning', which reflects my personal composing practice and research. This is dedicated to presence works that I refer to as 'Composition in Activism'. Here, activism is understood through its origins: the act of moving or thinking *(actus)* plus the practice of teaching/making *(ismos)*. Hence, the activist composer makes the listener think or act; s/he engages by creating the conditions to do so. As a curator, s/he makes visible, makes aware, connects, reconfigures, and reorganizes what already exists.[5] By doing so, the activist composer composes the guidebook for the work in the work itself. S/he curates through his own practice as a composer. Therefore, I consider the activist composer one who is engaged in a self-curating practice.[6]

4. Pierre Bourdieu, "The field of cultural production, or: The economic world reversed" in *Poetics,* volume 12, issues 4-5, November 1983, 311-356.

5. A curator in this context implies someone who deliberately puts different aesthetic objects together to create a cohesive narrative.

I share the idea of Hans Ulrich Gumbrecht that today's society is encountering a paradigm shift from a representation culture towards a presence culture. The musical concert becomes an immersive event, with the immediacy and the physicality of a theatre work.[7] Musicians become performers and composers become curators, and the audience is activated to formulate the answers or reformulate the questions the work proposes. In relation to this, musicologist Joep Christenhusz explains that listening has similarly reached a shift in focus: the conscious act of seeking to understand musical forms or structures has become a subpart of a broader, immersive experience, where meaning is "spread across the surface" instead of "hidden in the depth".[8]

In the advanced master program for contemporary music at KASK & Conservatory

6. Self-curation, or curation of the self, is an anthropological concept which has been studied with regard to social media and influencers, notably explicated by Erin B. Taylor in her 2014 essay "The Curation of the Self in the Age of the Internet". Taylor argues that the collections of objects we post on personal social media pages or Pinterest function as aesthetic forms to construct a social identity and express a narrative. In popular culture, these aesthetic forms are generally appropriated material culture forms (cloths, wearables, images, sounds, tastes). I adopted the concept of self-curation here for the activist composer, who deliberately makes use of aesthetic and material forms of a different nature, e.g. social relations, space, politics, circumstances, etc.
7. Hans Ulrich Gumbrecht, *Production of Presence—What Meaning Cannot Convey*, Stanford University Press, 2003. Gumbrecht argues that before this paradigm shift, the production of knowledge and meaning has been based upon the interpretation of the material world: extracting meaning from, or ascribing meaning to, the world around us. Now we have arrived at a presence-based approach to the world—one that is more concerned with the performance or presence of substance and reality than with the interpretation of it, and one where meaning is based on presence.
8. Joep Christenhusz, *Componisten van Babel*, Artez Press, 2016, 12, 14-15. Quotations translated by the author.

Ghent, for which I am the coordinator, the focal point for the students, who are among the contributors to this book, is the self-curation of their artistic practice and career. In accordance with the above-mentioned paradigm shift towards presence works, their musical practice marks a shift from an interpretive tradition of musical performance to performance as a relational and critical practice. Contemporary musicians, soloists, as well as ensembles and composers, therefore experiment with various forms of musical presentation and collaboration. In their quest to make their art and skills relevant to the world around them, they seek to act beyond their immediate field, searching for new impulses in other musical genres, related art forms, politics, and science, thus questioning the relevance of their work within a larger social context. Hence, the 'concert of the future', or indeed 'the concert of today', naturally includes transversal experimentation (with science, other arts, politics, ecology) and relational social dimensions (sharing, active participation). This activation and conditioning of various perspectives of the presentation practice—the physicality and performativity, the timeline, the location, the people involved (artists and visitors/listeners), the social relations and societal circumstances—is at the centre of self-curation as a practice.

To bring the principles of presence works, activist composition, and self-curation into practice, I was happy when, in the context of *CASC at KASK,* I was asked to co-organize a workshop with David Helbich, whose practice, in my view, also constitutes a proponent of presence works. The workshop eventually developed into an autonomous project: together, we initiated

House of Ear, a concept where sound is treated as a reflective exhibit on display for the visitor/listener to absorb, explore, and contemplate. Since GAME was at the same time invited to create a musical work for *Ear To The Ground Festival, House of Ear* became the obvious choice to be presented for this occasion.[9][10]

Joris Blanckaert

9. GAME is the Ghent Advanced Master Ensemble, the contemporary music ensemble that consists of the students of the advanced master program for contemporary music at KASK & Conservatory Ghent.
10. *Ear To The Ground* is a biennial festival dedicated to contemporary music, which is organized and hosted by Music Centre De Bijloke in Ghent. *House of Ear* was presented at the third in edition of 2019, April 6th.

Hearing is Intro-active; Listening is a Performative Act: introduction to *House of Ear*

Hearing has many spaces: the spaces far from our bodies, the space very close to our ears, the space on our ears and on our body's surfaces, the space inside our body, the space in our ear and our head, and the space of our imagination, our dreams, our thoughts, and our perception.

House of Ear is an exhibition concept that organizes a set of sound installations along the idea that both **hearing and listening are one process** that happens in all these spaces, inside and outside of our bodies.[11] In the masterclass that led to this exhibition, KASK & Conservatorium students, its organizers and I developed works that focused on one aspect of the hearing process that we divided into acoustic and experiential phenomena. What is sound? How does sound reach us? What does it tell us? And what do we add to sound ourselves?

House of Ear imagines the ear as a house. You can enter and walk through it, from room to room, all the way to the most hidden corner (let's say the basement, or the attic). In an ear-like fashion, the rooms and hallways of this house are organized in **a spiral formation,** as is the exhibition.

The visitors could start on either end. Walking up or down the spiral, they could follow the process

11. The experience of sound is triggered on the outside of our bodies by soundwaves (i.e. by the reflections, qualities, and movements of the sounds or us), and on the inside by inner body sounds resonances) thoughts, interpretations, memories, and imagination. Our ears are the sensors, translators and transformers of sound. In a spiral form, they accompany sound from the outside to the inside, with our eardrums popping in and out as if trying to negotiate between the inner and outer worlds by distributing the pressure equally. The complex properties of our ears make them quasi self-similar images of the entire disposition of hearing and listening.

of hearing and listening from the inside to the outside, or vice versa. On the outer end of the spiral, they find the world where sound waves travel through air, bounce back and forth between objects and surfaces, are absorbed and reflected; at the inner end of the spiral, they find what is left when waves are long gone: the traces that sound leaves in our thoughts.

As much as sounds can happen to us, as much as they can enter our body without any port being deliberately set open, we can also *imagine* sounds, think them. We can project our sound imaginations onto the world beyond our eardrums, as if we send them back out, against the draft of the incoming waves.

Hearing is an activity: sound activates more than just our eardrums, it triggers thoughts and impressions. We can finish a melody in our head, dream of a voice we know, or switch our focus. We can also deliberately cover our ears, with hands and earplugs (to change the proportion of the volume of outside and inside sounds) or headphones. We have a say in it.

We can literally change the way we hear, and also what we hear. I refer to the agency that lies in hearing as **intro-active.** This means that even in a seemingly passive state, as a mere listener of a concert, we actively co-create our experience.

The works in ***House of Ear*** search for ways to connect to this moment of **intro-activity** within the visitors, to shine light on it and ask it out for a dance. All works of the exhibition place a significant part of the outcome into the visitors' hands or ears.

With various strategies and techniques, the works create a dialogue with the audience's direct and individual experience. But instead of requiring an inter-active engagement, they emphasize the intro-active aspects of their proposals with **self-performance** concepts.

This method invites the visitor (audience member, listener, etc.) to participate in the work with the help of an instructional (or any other) form of guidance. The audience is the audience and the performer at the same time: they are both the player and the listener. The result of the audience's experience thus depends on various aspects: the guidance, the self-performance, and how both manage to spark an intro-active situation.

More than showing off creativity and originality, these works invite the audience to take agency, to be inspired by and use the art for their own needs. Thinking this through, it could mean that a work has to disappear to be fully there.

Noise can be heard as music.
Music can be heard as noise.
Listening is a performative act.

Self-performativity is a practice.
Yoga, flute, skateboard, language games are practices.
Practicing is a practice.

Listening also means attending.
Attending is a practice.
The space of the audience is a performative space.

David Helbich

House of Ear

Self-conditioning parcours by Anna Jalving, Philippe Druez, Hugo Ranilla de Castro, Anne Zeuwts, Heike Langsdorf, Clara Levy, Joanneke Jouwsma, Joris Blanckaert, Simone Basani, Noriko Yakushiji, Sara Méndez, Ward Ginneberge, Mar Sala Romagosa, David Helbich

You enter the building through two heavy glass doors.

The room you enter is big and the hard stone floor makes your steps echo along with your movement. The building consists of both the old part, dating back to the 17th century, and the new part, built in glass and steel. You walk up two flights of a staircase of glass. At the end of the stairs, there is a chair for you and a pair of headphones. You put on the headphones and the sound that reaches your ears takes you back to the entrance, where you were just moments ago. However, it is as if sounds that were in the background are now in the foreground and amplified. The mumbling sound of a vacuum cleaner blends in with the hum of an air conditioner, a soft echo of steps on a nearby set of stairs, and the voices of people that you cannot see.

In Your Hands

This piece will be composed by you through listening and listing the sounds that you hear.

For this piece, you either could produce sounds yourself—for example by playing (with) concrete objects—or use sounds that you hear or even imagine.

First, identify the sounds that catch your ear.

List them in order to be able to separate and think of them. This way, you can choose how to compose in your mind with your specific selection of sounds.

By mixing and overlapping sounds in your imagination, you can let certain sound features be amplified and cancel others out.

You will make music out of what we normally would not conceive as worthwhile to listen to.

List these sounds in order to compose little groups of three sounds at a time.

Take your time to create this piece for your own enjoyment.

You are the selector, composer, performer, and listener of this piece.

To get into the mood, you could listen for these little groups of sounds:

The buzzing of a fridge the wind
the noise of a passing train

the wind a passing train a bird twitters

the voices of children passing by birds singing
your steps

steps in the hallway echoing the voices of children

a key turning in your front door lock breath
water running

a dog barking a vacuum cleaner a pen on paper
rain

builders on lunch break a plane
leaves caught in the wind

While you climb the three-floor staircase enclosed in a substantial transparent cage of glass windows, your gaze is drawn outside to the 14th century red brick buildings from the former abbey and hospital. The inside and the outside merge through the glass walls: reflections of trees, doors, stairs, buildings, the courtyard, and people. You notice that sound reflects and mixes in the same way as the views do, and you become aware of the sound of children playing.

Once you reach the top floor and enter the exhibition space, you observe an art installation in the middle of the foyer. A four-meter-high tripod. You read on the leaflet that it contains a mechatronic system with two ultrasonic transducer array discs. A guide approaches you and tells you that the discs are able to beam inaudible sound in all directions. Now you notice that, in this room, the children's voices don't come from outside, but from the interior.

The guide says "the beams appear as sound bounced back from the spots they hit on the glass and on concrete walls". Then she smiles and walks away.

How and why do I create space for sonic reflection?

A possible answer comes from a vibrant sound memory that pops up from time to time—a specific experience I had while windsurfing. When the wind conditions are right (not that good for exciting windsurfing, though) I could sometimes hear conversations emanating from the beach, a few kilometers from where I was at sea. The shape of the sail formed by the wind acted as a parabolic reflector, situating my ears as the focal point. I could direct the sail and tune in to sounds of vivacious beachgoers, a distant radio, or conferring petanque players.

It must have been my tinnitus that, at one point, changed my path of thinking, exploring, and creating a predominantly visual world towards that of the sonic. Tinnitus is not just a high pitch or buzzing; people hear all sorts of things. Someone told me she sometimes hears children playing in her head. This is a mild and acute form of tinnitus.

It is curious for me to notice that when I wander through the neighbourhoods of my city, I'm always beguiled by the sound of cheerful children at school playgrounds during their breaks. It's kind of comforting and energizing to me.

In Your Hands

When I created the *Kindergarten* installation, it fulfilled all my expectations, and soon its value as a universal system became clear. I extended the use of two sound beams aiming in different directions and added the electromechanical movement to get the sense of dispersal. I extended the stand-alone installation with an audio input, MIDI and CV (control voltage for modular synthesizers) interface, thereby transforming it to an instrumental device under the name of *The Radison*.

If you are curious to experience similar sound reflections to the ones of the *Kindergarten* installation, you could 'create' them analogically: you could try to go surfing, sit in a courtyard, or just walk freely through the streets. Check where you are in different moments: are there conditions for sonic reflection? If there are, are you lucky enough to actually hear reflections?

If you want to try to realize a similar sound installation, you could use two identical systems, operating independently. The core of each system is an Arduino processor with an SD-card reader, a custom-built sound board, and a parametric ultrasonic transducer array connected to two tiny servo motors.

When running, the software program calculates in real time the rotation positions, based on an algorithm. The values are, to some extent, random, but rather organic, reflecting the movement of children in a playground. Movement of the motors is restricted to predefined settings to limit the horizontal (pan or x-axis) and vertical (tilt or y-axis) movement within the hemispheres to create ideal reflection angles (Figure B).

I recorded the children's playing sounds at elementary school playgrounds in my neighborhood. I only used the mono sound for the samples stored on the SD-card. They are different in length and are selected and played randomly by the program (Figure A).

The sound beam system consists of 100 ultrasonic piezo transducers. The precisely mounted array modulates the sound on an almost non-diverging carrier, bringing the inaudible sound to a surface where it is 'demodulated' and becomes audible.

Figure A

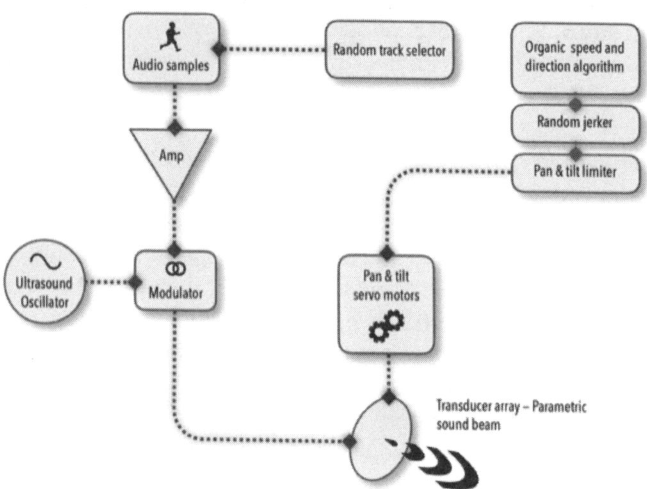

Figure B

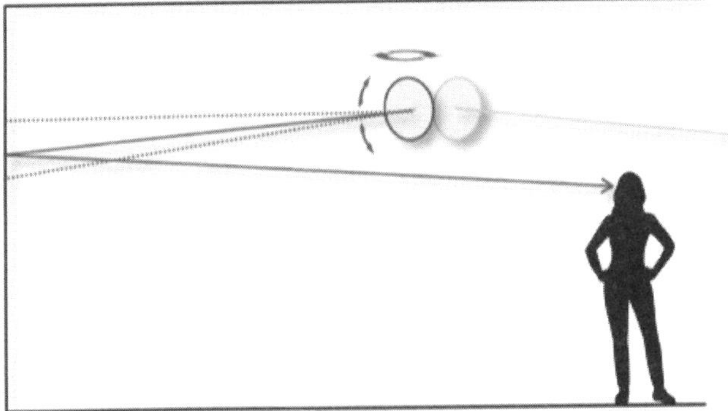

(H)EAR HERE

Anne Zeuwts & Hugo Ranilla de Castro

In the long corridor connecting all the rooms of House of Ear, *you find 17 frames displayed like paintings in a museum. You see different materials and objects inside the frames. They accompany your path through* House of Ear. *As you hold your ear against the framed materials, they reveal different sounds, textures, and sensations going from sounds produced by your inner body to those stemming from the different materials themselves.*

Throughout the corridor, you see spectators/ participants listening to and feeling the framed objects. Some of the objects have obvious sound qualities, such as dry leaves, aluminium foil, or a kitchen timer that might evoke different feelings or long-forgotten memories. Others are less defined or expectable. You might wonder: what are the sound qualities of a soft sponge? Can steel wool produce a warm tingly noise? What does it feel like to press your ear against cold metal? Will it have a cold sound as well, or a cold lack of sound instead?

We are surrounded by sounds all the time. The constant flow makes us selective to some of the interesting qualities of these sounds and numb to others. *(H)Ear Here* aims to canalize the sound flow in order to make us more conscious of our auditory surroundings.

Throughout the book, connecting the works of the other contributors, the reader will find three sets of (H)Earing exercises.

Each of these correspond to a division of the human ear:

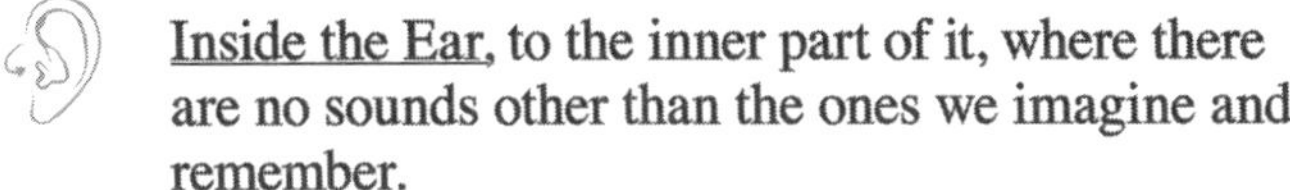

Inside the Ear, to the inner part of it, where there are no sounds other than the ones we imagine and remember.

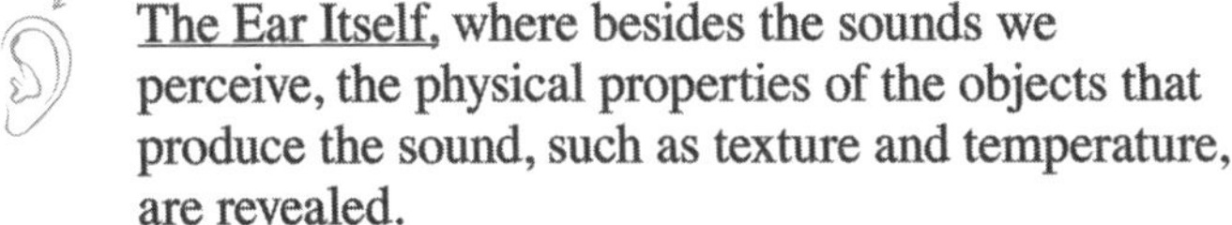

The Ear Itself, where besides the sounds we perceive, the physical properties of the objects that produce the sound, such as texture and temperature, are revealed.

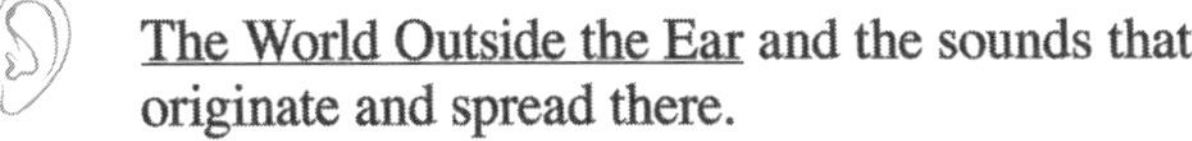

The World Outside the Ear and the sounds that originate and spread there.

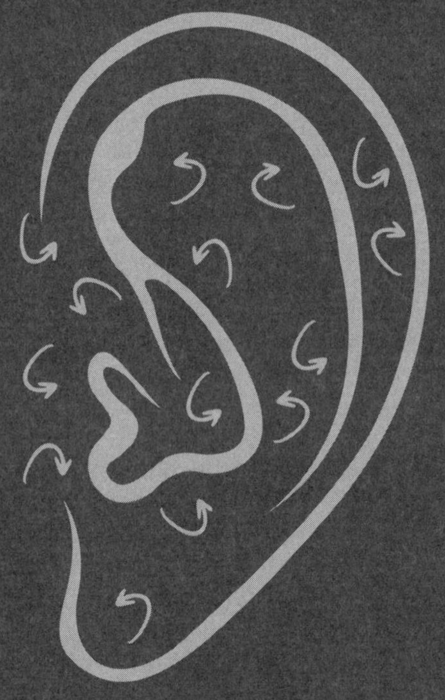

Hugo Ranilla de Castro & Anne Zeuwts

INSIDE THE EAR — IMAGINATION

Take a look to your left. Choose an object you see.
It can be anything you want: a window, a piece of clothing, this book…

> Imagine the sound it would make if you pressed your ear against it.

> Imagine feeling the surface touching your ear.

Now hold your ear against the chosen object and compare the reality to what you imagined.

The corridor is long and there are doors on both sides. It gradually curves to the left, so you cannot see the end of it. As you start walking down the corridor, you hear some noise of crockery coming from the first door on your right. You enter the door and you find yourself in a home environment. Objects symbolize different rooms: a carpet for the living room, a single bed for the bedroom. An artist is engaged in producing sounds of cooking with pots and water. You notice that the sound she is producing becomes abstract once in a while. Another artist gently fans the face of a blindfolded spectator, while simultaneously shaking a necklace behind her own back. What will the blindfolded spectator imagine?

Rum-erra-torium was all about adjusting 'stuff' in such a way that one would think 'something' is (in) the room.

When configuring *Rum-erra-torium*, we found ourselves immersed in the vast realm of improvisation. In particular, we entered a rather specific explorative field: foley sound art. We indulged in linking things and places we had at hand to things and places we were imagining and which we wanted to evoke.

We treated any object as an instrument, which meant that we had to condition ourselves first—i.e. to learn to sense these objects in different ways.

- Attune your listening and hearing.

- Find plausible connections between your sonic-spatial memory and your imagination.

- What does it need to *make* the sound this bird is making in that tree?
- What does it need, for example, to *suggest* we are walking in the snowy landscape?

- Understand what kind of materials and which way of handling them can suggest a certain imagined place.

- Explore this as a virtuous activity of dedicated hearing and imagining: how can you cause that which you want to resonate in space?

- How do you need to move and manipulate a ‘thing’ so that it suggests what you imagine?

- Open up to what surrounds you.
- Open not only your ears, but simultaneously your sense for the visual and for movement.

- Grasp your instantly available abilities: transpose, translate, and transform what you once heard and now remember into the audible shared space!

- Remember: it takes one evocative sound image to imagine a whole landscape.

We would like to thank the Foley Artists Community for sharing some of their tricks with us.

MATERIALS	PLACES / EVENTS
pot full of water	fish in the river
toothpicks	mice in the bedroom
straw chair	walking through dry leaves and branches
polystyrene	glacier breaking apart in the Alps
aluminium foil and / or thermic blanket	campfire
heavy ball rolling	stormy weather
grains falling	rain
grains in a moving tube	beach
maïzena under stepping shoes	snowy landscape
two drinking glasses held against the ears	inside a space shuttle
thin rope turning fast	birds in the sky
velvet fabric	________
water dripping from the tap	________
hairdryer	________
radio, set between two frequences	________
squash getting chopped	________
cracking leather	________
paper leaves rubbing against each other	________
electric boiler	________
________	bees foraging
________	bees dying
________	silent protest
________	sailing through the canal
________	bicycles on cobblestones
________	night sky without city lights
________	windless desert
________	never ending traffic jam

WALK.THROUGH / THROW.BACK / ARRIVAL.TIME

Joanneke Jouwsma

There is a small, half-darkened room. The door of the room is open. You enter. There are several projections to see. During 'Walk.Through', *a young woman is standing in a vast landscape. She stands with her back turned to the camera and slowly rolls out a paper ribbon. The paper falls down beside her and is occasionally blown by the soft wind. At the bottom of the image of* 'Throw.Back', *two arms suddenly appear with blue sleeves and hands full of sheets of paper. The paper is thrown into the air in a short movement. The arms remain suspended in the air for a short stretch, while the paper whirls down. In* 'Arrival. Time', *the sky is blue with a lilac tinge over it. Just as suddenly as in* 'Throw.Back', *a paper ribbon is waving through the air making a loop. At a high speed, the paper falls down. In all the videos it is almost windless; the paper sighs along a breath of wind that may or may not be there. The young woman's hair dances from time to time; the blades of grass swing slowly and the sky is bright blue. All sounds of the videos have different melodies that follow one another. The birds sing, a train passes in the distance, the wind rustles, the paper crackles, creaks, and falls.*

For these works I have practiced with a series of accidental sounds that, together, form a composition.

paper

arms

sheets of

hands and

a paper ribbon is

crackling

another paper ribbon skims along the empty air

typhoon one long signal

the paper strokes

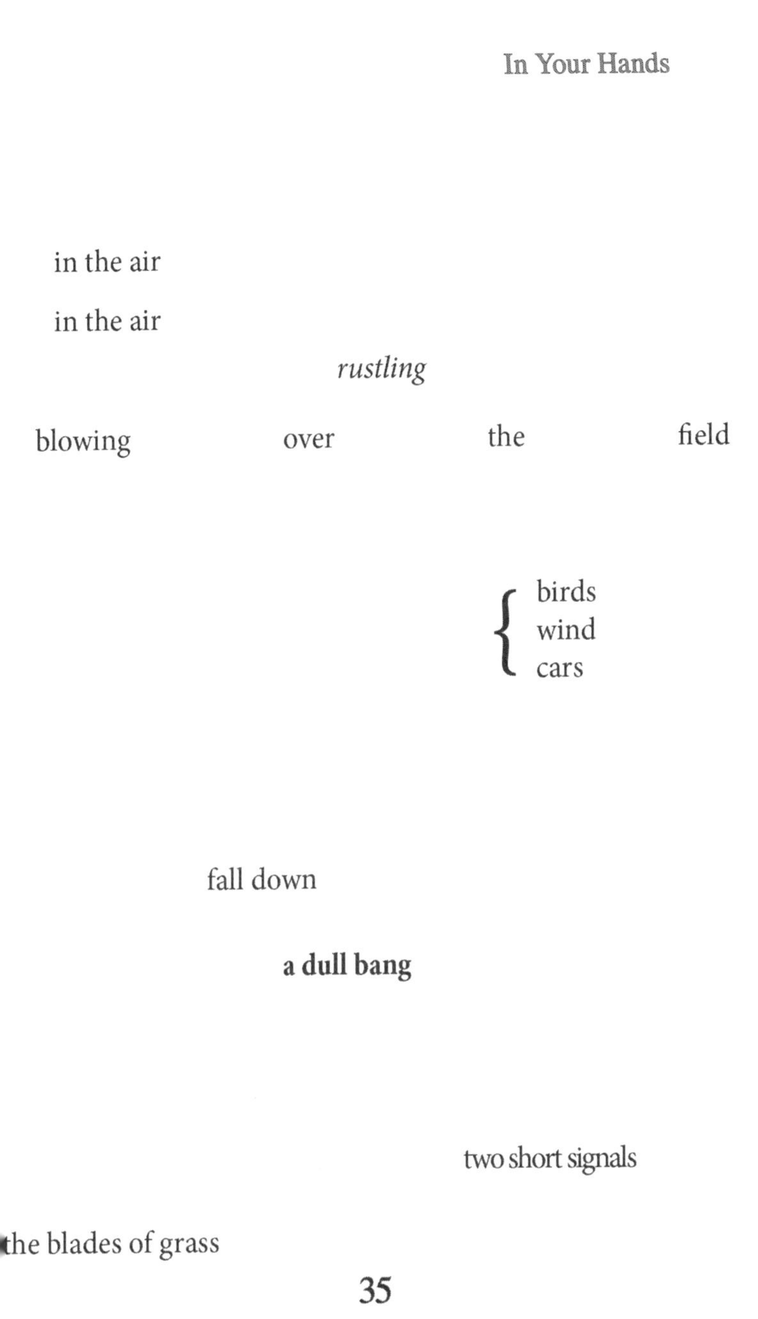

in the air

in the air

rustling

blowing over the field

{ birds
wind
cars

fall down

a dull bang

two short signals

the blades of grass

RE:FLECTION

Joris Blanckaert

You enter an almost empty room that is dark and quiet. Against one of the walls you see a giant mirror with a hypersensitive rattan armchair in front of it. Next to it, there is small side table on top of which lie a book, headphones, and an illuminated globe. The chair invites you to sit down, look in the mirror, and put on the headphones. Different voices are gently reading the same short text in many different languages. It seems to be an important text and you sit very quietly for its entire duration in order not to be disturbed by your own movements and noises. Any movement that rustles the chair (tapping your fingers, crossing your legs, a restless foot, even breathing), are amplified in the headphones to an annoying level. The text is explaining what is actually happening at the very moment: the politics of unwanted sounds or noise.

RE:flection: listen to the sounds we produce and the impact they may have on our environment.

In Your Hands

Silence is precious. Silence is curious. Silence is scarce. In the environment where I live and work (schools, theatres, coffee bars, the city center, my home office) it is, in my opinion, people and their tools and toys that produce most of the often unwanted sounds. These sounds invade other people's personal acoustic bubbles, and RE:flection could help to make people aware of, and reflect on, the impact their physical presence might have on the acoustic ecosystem.

What is RE:flection?

RE:flection is a minimally invasive method to increase sonic self-awareness.

How to use RE:flection and in what circumstances

Collect three or more low-density polyethylene plastic bags, i.e. the (not so) good old (semi-)transparent plastic trash can bags. Put the bag under your clothes against your back, belly, and bottom. In a more adventurous version, you may consider crafting underwear out of the bags. For better results, the bottom plastic bag may be replaced by bubble wrap.

Put a wrapped candy or toffee in your pocket.

Go to a public building where people are sitting and where one needs to be quiet, i.e. the reading room of a public library, a church with people praying, or a psychiatrist's waiting room. It is key to walk at a brisk pace in order to raise your heart rate and the intensity of your breathing. Once inside the place, sit next to someone who is concentratedly fulfilling the purpose of the space: reading, praying, waiting, etc. Carefully sit down, take the candy out of your pocket, and gently unwrap it. While the candy melts in your mouth, you might attempt not to make any noise, while at the same time trying to discern at least a dozen different noises surrounding you. Listen.

When to stop using RE:flection

As soon as the candy is gone, leave the place quietly, take out the plastic, and continue your life.

THE HOUSE WE HAVE BUILT

Simone Basani

You hear someone talking behind a slightly open door. The voice seems to be intent on explaining something. You get closer: it sounds like it is describing a place. The description doesn't proceed smoothly though; sometimes, it gets interrupted by strange noises. You decide to enter. There are two spectators. They listen to a performer who is in front of them. It seems as if the performer is trying to reconstruct through his memory the apartment where he grew up as a child. He invites you and the other spectators to visualize that apartment in the room you are currently in. He walks across the invisible apartment, while pointing at—or directly transforming himself into—those features that are stuck in his memory: architectural details, and material or immaterial objects.

Sometimes he replaces the names of the objects (plants, mirrors, corridors, ceilings …) with names of actions he remembers. For instance, 'doors' become 'whispers', 'floor' becomes 'growling'. You notice that his voice changes when he names those actions; it becomes the actions he remembers. Or maybe it is the emotional-psychological grain of those actions that takes over his voice.

How to host inside your voice the grain, the density of a relationship you have with a place?

Especially when:

1. it is a complicated, long-standing relationship, charged with memory, time, and emotions;

2. you want to make an audience understand the story of that relationship.

Choose a place that has been part of your life, where you don't go so often anymore, or that is even inaccessible for one reason or another.

Think of three spots in that place that have been marked by events that are still stuck in your memory. Visualize them.

Choose one.

Hold this thought for a moment before continuing.

Then ask yourself: how was the materiality of the specific spot you chose involved in that event that you still remember?

Did something fall down, fly away, or touch your or another's body during that event?

What about the materiality of your reaction to that event: was there heavy breathing, singing, crying, yelling … ? What about their rhythm?

Listen to what your body remembers of that event, and especially of your reactions to it. You are not inventing the sound for an object, nor are you even trying to recreate your voice as a child, for instance.

Rather, you are listening to the auditive and tactile traces that are still stored in your body. Choose the clearest ones. They speak of the physical and emotional relationship that still exists between you and the matter of those memories.

But how to let an audience enter this troubled soundscape?

Guide yourself again across that place. Visit those spots you remember one by one. Please forget their proper names.

Remember how your body calls them. What is the language (if it is a language at all)?

Let that word or sound come out.

Stay with that sound. Is it a repetitive one? How does it evolve? Does it break too easily?

Acknowledge when it happens, and acknowledge when a common object you remember becomes something else through sound.

When a bush becomes the feeling of a bee sting on your hand, and its name a hissing sucked in between your teeth.

When a curtain becomes a dark 'twwoooooommmm' and your voice becomes suddenly very low, or when you walk around the perimeter of a table and every step you take is a word of a poem that you are trying to memorize, when a garden becomes the moment when you have a cut on your leg and you press around it and blow on it while singing a song meant to send the pain away, when a floor becomes a moment of anger, when soil, plants, and vases are thrown from outside to inside the house, when a ceiling becomes a high shout that reaches all the neighbours' apartments, the one on your floor and the one above, when a locked door, that shouldn't be closed, becomes the whispers you utter to convince someone to open it…

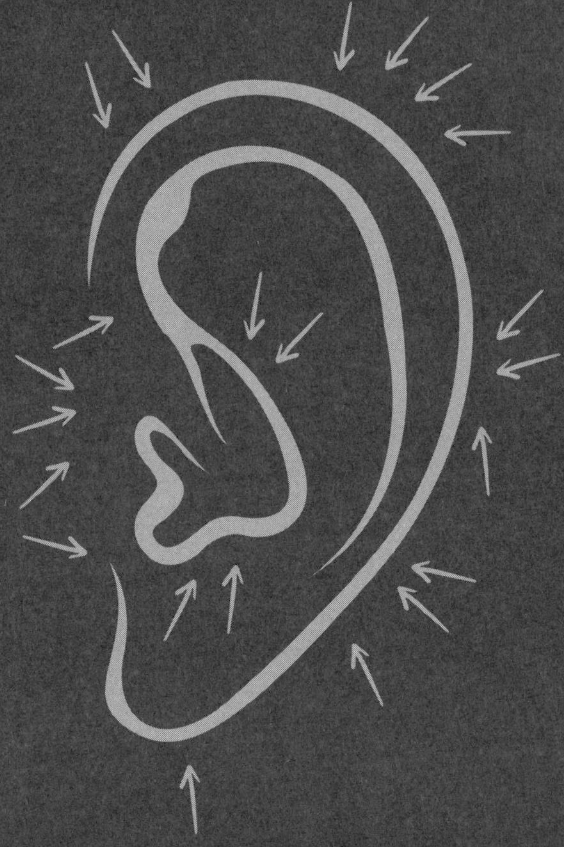

Hugo Ranilla de Castro & Anne Zeuwts

THE EAR ITSELF — TEXTURES AND SOUNDS

Pick an item from one of the following lists:

When you are inside
A drink from your fridge
A sponge (dry or slightly wet)
A sheet of aluminium foil
A plastic bag
Your own hair

When you are outside
A bunch of leaves (dried or fresh)
A log or the trunk of a tree
A road sign
A rock
Grass

Put your ear against the item.

Observe the sensation of touch:
the temperature and the texture.

Observe the sound:
when you try to stay as still as possible, and
when you move the object against your ear.

Look for the most pleasant texture to feel, and the most pleasant texture to listen to.

BEYOND THE DOOR… YOUR PERSONAL SOUND

Noriko Yakushiji

In the middle of your exhibition visit, you are invited to step into the bathroom and press your ear against the toilet doors (let's leave aside whether that is decent or not). You press your ear against the two toilet doors and notice that you can hear sounds through them.

The use of a surface transducer (a special speaker that makes any connected surface vibrate along with a sound) ensures that the sound can only be enjoyed by pressing an ear against the doors. They lead you to sounds and songs of two different cities. The first door lets you listen to Ostend, a seaside town, the second one to Shibuya, a much louder city.

In March 2019, I made sound recordings at the pedestrian scrambles crossing the urban districts of Shibuya in Tokyo, Japan, and between the sandy beaches of Ostend in Belgium. The two places would become the soundworld beyond the doors of my installation at *House of Ear* (2019).

The noise of Shibuya was as loud as I imagined it would be, but there were more sounds than I expected on the sandy beaches of Ostend. I was surprised to hear seagulls, waves, and children's playful sounds with such dynamics.

I felt clearly the coexistence of my inner sounds and the ones around my body.

I came to the realization that the sounds that surround me all the time can have a relationship to my inner voice, or my personal sounds. They can be mixed with each other.

The experience of mixing inner and outside sounds is similar to watching a raging storm, huddled up inside your house.

Both sheltered by your house and in the midst of this outside noise, the sounds from within (conducted through the bones) are more clearly audible.

The following score makes you experience exactly this.

In Your Hands

Take a pair of earplugs or headphones that close tightly around your ears. If you don't have any, you can always use your own fingers.

Step outside.

Go to a place that is as noisy as possible—for example, the nightlife downtown in an Asian city. If that's not an option, I'd suggest a club or the busiest shopping district!

Put on your earplugs or headphones or stick your fingers into your ears, and take a deep breath. The sound of your breathing should dominate the noise around you.

Once you get used to this, try humming with your mouth closed while exhaling.

Now, sing or hum songs or melodies.

As your skull—your 'house'—amplifies your voice for your inner ear, you will see how little effort and volume you need to produce sound.

No one will notice what is pretty loud for yourself.

Enjoy your very personal amplifier!

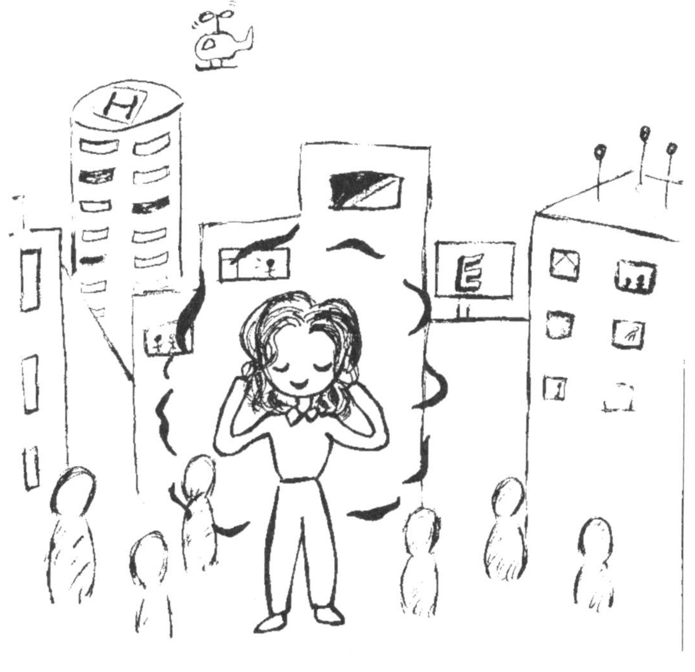

You enter a room with very little light. The space is quite empty. It is small, with four smooth walls and a door. A closed door that you're not going to open. There's a person sitting behind a table waiting for you. She has long, very dark, smooth hair. She is calm and smiling, and she attracts you with a confident look to enter safely into this unknown space. On the table lie a computer, a small lamp, and headphones.

She says: "Hi! Welcome to this room! Please, take a seat". And while you listen to her, you sit down and put the headphones on. Silence. In that moment, you don't hear anything coming from your headphones.

However, the girl in front of you continues talking to you. "I'm thinking now about the situation. You and me, sitting in front of each other. Actually, it could be any situation: a visit to the doctor, a meeting with your boss, an appointment to sign a residence permit …"

Without noticing, you are paying attention to a stranger and everything becomes confusing because you don't know what course this conversation will take.

She continues her speech: "As writer Cristina Rivera says, 'migrating' is the great verb of our times. Are you from here?"

Confused, you shyly answer, and at the same time you hear a voice coming from the headphones, interrupting the dialogue you are having with the person in front of you: "Her accent is not from here, is it? You might wonder: where did it come from? It's not her, it's deeper, it sounds like a man's, right?"

The girl at the table continues to talk: "Although migration is one …";

But you cannot stop listening to the voice in the headphones. It is as if it were your own thoughts, your inner voice, battling with yourself and questioning the topic the woman is talking about. To be able to continue paying attention gets harder and even stressful, unpleasant … because all you want is to be aware of where everything you hear comes from.

In Your Hands

Next time you are in a conversation, analyze the process of listening. Are your ears trained? Imagine a situation in which the other speaker is from a foreign country, has a thick accent, or even misses sounds. At first, you'll be attentive and focused. However, as the conversation progresses, your mind will start to go somewhere else, and your inner voice will start commenting.

That moment of escape is what interests me. Let's now analyze why it happens, or where it leads. What do you hear? Are you able to tell?

Remember that the conversation is still flowing, and your mind is struggling to pay attention …

You want to be attentive; what lack of respect if you were not! But the inner voice commenting on the situation is still there, disrupting your focus all the time. Or rather … what disrupts what?

Did you perhaps already know what you are listening to?

Even if you want to find out, the end result will be stressful and overwhelming, and might even affect your mood. There is too much information, too much to pay attention to. Well, have you understood anything at the end?

What would you have preferred to hear: data that is given to you in a simple way or your own thoughts?

Do you know your inner voice and how to manage the moment when it exceeds your attention? Do you usually listen to it?

If so, how can you keep yourself *pensante* in such a situation? How can you remain a thinking human being able to separate the different layers of sound and information that reach your ears?

AS DELICATE AS A DIAPHRAGM OR ANOTHER PACE

Joanneke Jouwsma

In a room, numerous white paper dresses hang from a clothes rack. When you walk past the dresses, the air makes them move and sound.

You see a performer walking towards the dresses. She takes one off the clothes rack. She carefully puts the dress down in front of her feet and removes the hanger. While she is crouching, she puts her arms inside the bottom of the dress. She slowly rises up and gently squirms herself into the paper dress.

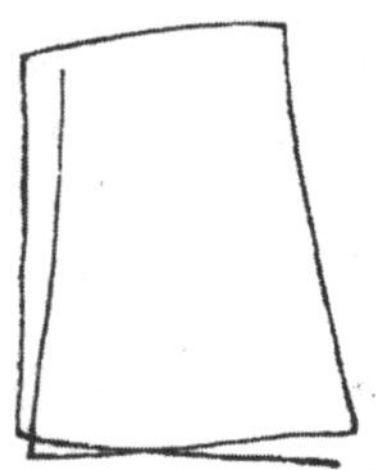

The movement of the paper creates a 'deafening' sound from the inside. The paper is cracking and tearing. When she is wearing the dress, she takes a step forward. The dress is rustling. She sets one step after the other. She slowly walks by. The white paper dresses are like a membrane: a thin skin that is worn by a performer and vibrates because of her movements.

Take a piece of paper as long as your body and as wide as your shoulders. Make a cut-out in the middle the size of your head. Put on the paper dress and walk very slowly through a landscape for a long period of time.

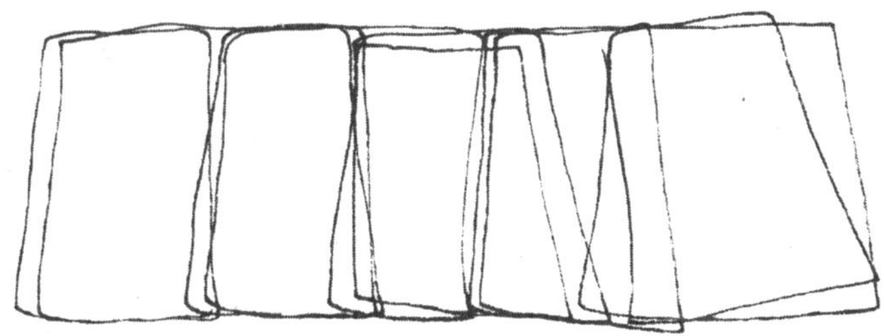

SILENT / SONIC MEDITATION

Ward Ginneberge

You enter a small room. It is dimly lit with an Edison lightbulb placed on a low side table. Two leather chairs are facing each other, turned slightly sideways. On a small desk in the back of the room some papers, stationery, and three small cactuses are organized in an orderly fashion. You are welcomed to take a seat in one of the chairs. In one of the other chairs sits a performer. He asks you to participate in a short meditation that he will read to you. The focus of the meditation is to imagine the sounds that are described to you. It is suggested to you that you can close your eyes during the meditation. "Try to listen with your inner ear".

In Your Hands

Our imagination is the (unlicensed) therapist of our soul. Through meditation, we can calm our nervous system to give way to our mind.

Ask someone to read the following meditation for you.
If this is not possible, do it by yourself.
The reader should use a calm pacing to leave room for imagination.

Be amazed by the sounds that are stored there and the possibility to imagine new ones.

If you listen to it, close your eyes.
This prescription will reach your inner ear:

"Imagine the voice of a friend
Imagine the voice of a friend calling your name
It sounds desperate
It sounds loving
It sounds angry
It sounds impatient

Imagine the voice of your friend through a megaphone
Imagine the voice of your friend through a face mask
Imagine the voice of your friend with their face pushed into the ground
It sounds desperate
It sounds helpless
It sounds hoarse

Imagine the voice of your friend when you are embracing each other
Imagine the voice of your friend whispering in your ear
It sounds kind

Imagine the sounds you heard the last time you walked somewhere without social distancing
Imagine those sounds 1.5 meters away
Imagine the sounds of people calling you names
Imagine the sounds of people marching alongside you

Imagine the sounds of a walk with your friend
How does it sound?"

COMPOSING SOUNDS AS AUTONOMOUS OBJECTS IN A SCRIPTED SPACE

Mar Sala Romagosa

You walk into a sort of bathroom. A monitor is displaying moving images. You see headphones and you put them on. The video installation makes you watch and listen to found footage and sound field recordings. You ask yourself: what hat exactly am I seeing? What do I listen to?

What comes out of the headphones makes one imagine sonic spaces while watching images looping, not necessarily associated with each other. Offering neither a beginning nor end of a sequence, the video and sound editing suggest that you stay as long as is bearable and/or desired. For how long are you still available?

The interest in this work comes out of my personal practice of listening to sounds in a loop, over and over again. Over and over again, sensing their materiality. In this way, I can develop a sense for their complexity and experience their beauty. Otherwise, they just pass too fast; they fade away. So, recordings and repetitively playing back sounds is my way of 'holding onto' what otherwise disappears in a rush. It also reveals the musicality, or the potential musicality, that lies in every raw sound.

For the installation described above, I worked with what I found 'on site'. The idea is to never extend material too far; no specific associations need to be made.

What is necessary is that the ear has enough time, regardless of what it imagines while hearing, to listen to everything—everything coming and becoming something else through imagination. This way, we can make inaudible things audible.

I will start listening to my surroundings here, sitting in a village in Catalunya, during the second wave of Covid 19. You can follow my listening experience while you read. You can listen to it too, through your imagination.

At the end, when listening brings me to smelling, please continue listening … and if you like, continue this text by using the sounds that you are listening to at this moment.

> I hear a wave … a wave that comes back … I wonder if, after a while, they will all start sounding the same …
> I now hear footsteps … footsteps that are breaking the water … the waves keep on … they fade in and out, I hear the footsteps one last time …
>
> I remember the waves, another sound layer joins, some birds fighting for food, the water breaks again. The waves are now mixing with the birds fighting for food.
>
> The wind changes direction … I can hear it whistling … I wonder if the birds can also hear … This wind that makes the waves fade … Can I still hear them? … Maybe I am just remembering the waves while the wind keeps blowing in my ears …

The sound of this whistle is dominating everything, dominating everything for quite a while as the water impacts between the rocks … for a while the wind … the whistling sound now moves, moves away, slowly, then faster, getting less loud, softer … suddenly stopping.

I remember when it stopped suddenly I could hear the footsteps again … suddenly they were on the sand, no more water splashing, a totally new sort of sound. The water moving fluently while the hectic footsteps remain …

Strangely, now I also hear the voice of the people behind me … and the way the wind blocks my hearing again …

But this time, I realize that the waves are gone, the light is fading, and the whistling is growing.

The smell of the sea … the landscape changed … the sea is calmer … the voices are gone, and I let my sound memories come to me …

It starts to rain … the smell is stronger while the waves move and come back to life … like they never stopped …

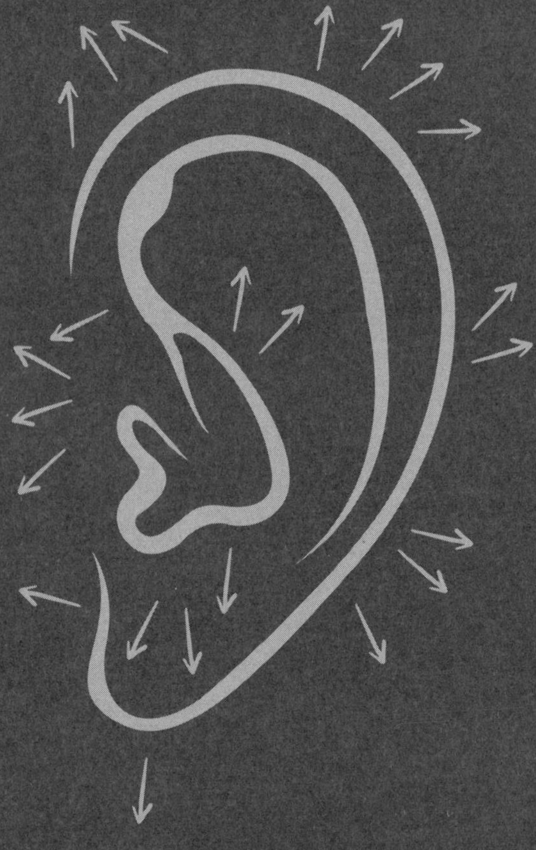

Hugo Ranilla de Castro & Anne Zeuwts

OUTSIDE THE EAR — SURROUNDING SOUNDS

Reach an outdoor place where you feel comfortable.

Take one minute and listen carefully to the sound of your surroundings. You can close your eyes if you want to. What exactly do you hear?

Focus on the sounds that are more dominant.

Concentrate now on the subtler sounds.

Try to find any sounds whose source you do not understand. Any sounds you have never noticed before.

Repeat the process. Focus on the sounds of nature:

listen to the birds, the wind, the plants …

Now focus on sounds made by humans:

listen to conversations, laughter, clapping, people walking or running.

Listen carefully again and put your attention on mechanical sounds this time:

are there cars passing by or honking their horns?

Now try listen to whether there is construction on a street nearby.

Switch again. Concentrate on the sound of the conversations or laughter you heard before. Could they come from a TV or a radio?

You enter an empty space. Depending on how tall you are, you hear a loud or less loud tone that fills the room. The tone changes slowly, cross-fades into other tones, intervals … On the far end of the long space stands a black shiny box: a subwoofer. It looks a bit like a miniature version of the monolith on 2001: A Space Odyssey. *On the floor lie some tape stripes in different colours and three roles of tape.*

You see other visitors walking through the room very slowly, suddenly standing still, moving their heads back and forth, and then taking a piece of tape and marking the floor with it.

A text on the wall invites the visitors to walk slowly through the room and listen to the volume changes in the tones. The moment they have the feeling they found 'the most silent' spot, they mark that spot on the floor with some tape and continue the 'silent-spot-hunt'.

The difference in volume is caused by the standing (sound) waves of the sine tone composition from the speaker.[12]

The soft and loud spots of these tones are measurable regularities and a natural phenomenon directly related to the frequencies of the soundwaves. The composition uses only frequencies where the standing sound waves have their peaks every 40 to 400 cm. These positions are stable as long as the same tone is still playing. With each change of tone, the grid of volume peaks (soft or loud) changes, as do the positions of the visitors.

12. In physics, a standing wave, also known as a stationary wave, is a wave which oscillates in time, but whose peak amplitude profile does not move in space. https://en.wikipedia.org/wiki/Standing_wave#:~:text=In%20physics%2C%20a%20standing%20wave,the%20wave%20are%20in%20phase (last access on March 18, 2021).

On your phone or computer, search for a video (or sound file) with a long version of the frequency 440Hz.

For example, on YouTube. This is the frequency that musicians often use to tune their instruments, so you will find it easily. Play back the video on full volume and leave your device on a table or a surface that is not too low.

Now, walk around slowly in your room and listen carefully to the slight differences in the volume of the tone.

Each time that you have the feeling that the tone reaches its loudest volume, leave a trace, an object, or a mark on that point on the ground.

If it works out well, you will find the objects on the ground with distances of approximately 77 cm between them.